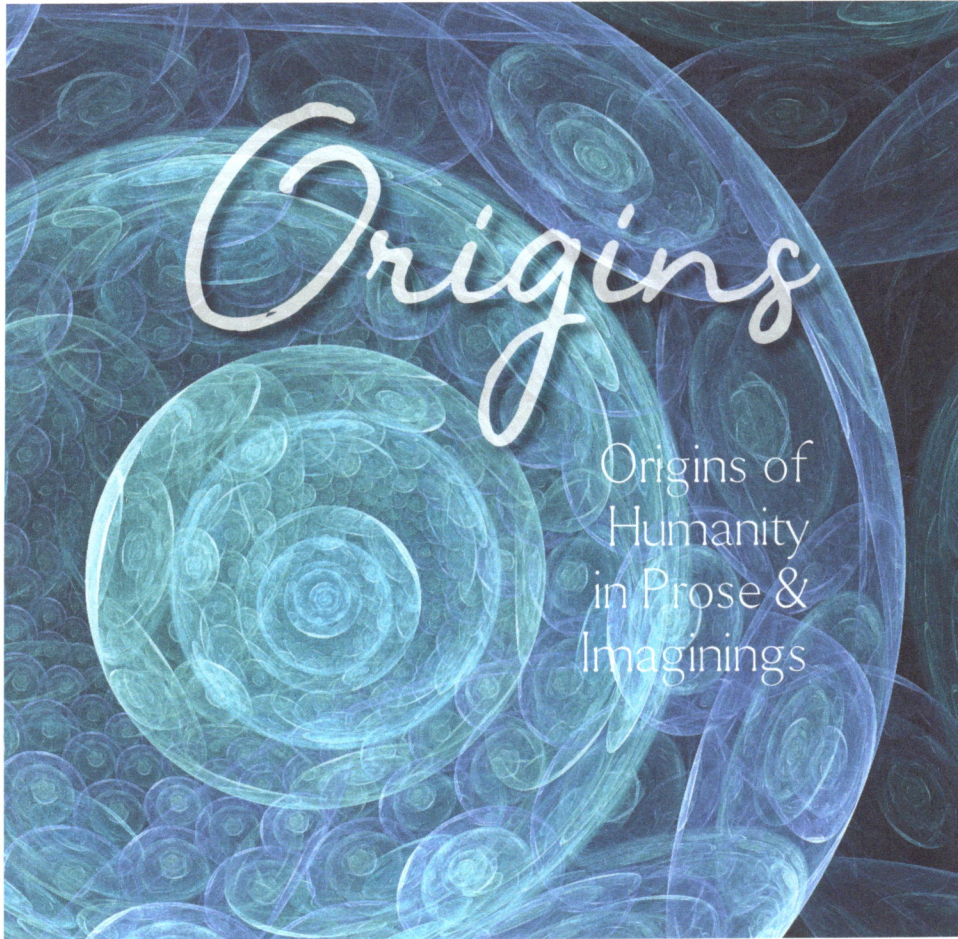

Origins

Origins of Humanity in Prose & Imaginings

JULIE RENEE DOERING

Origins of Humanity in Prose & Imaginings
Copyright ©2019 by Julie Renee Doering

ISBN-13: 978-1-7333024-0-1

Gable-Kennedy Publications
PO Box 549
Carmel Valley, California 93924

Info@Julierenee.com

Printed in the U.S.A.

Book design and cover: Michelle Radomski
www.onevoicecan.com

Warning – Disclaimer

The purpose of this book is to educate and entertain. The author and/or publisher does not guarantee that anyone following the techniques, suggestions, tips, ideas or strategies will become successful. The author and/or publisher shall have neither liability nor responsibility to anyone with respect to any loss or damage caused, or alleged to be caused, directly by the information in this book.

Endorsement – Disclaimer

Reference herein to any specific commercial products, process, or service by trade name, trademark, manufacturer, or otherwise, in no manner endorses or sponsors the products, processes or offerings.

Where did we come from?

Where did we come from as human and angelic spirits? Have you wondered why we are the way we are, and how we're related to the Angels and God? Why do they love us and shepherd us? Who are we in the grand scheme of life?

We'll begin an exploration of our origins through poetry and revelation. And take a visually pleasing journey through the sacred passages in this text as we discover our true nature and how we came to be here on planet earth. Living, loving and expressing in the most extraordinary ways.

I remember a time when it was not
When all that was
Was what could not be
When who was all
And I was we.
When I existed as we
We were a blaze.
The fire was power
The light was life
And I was not
Alone did not exist
                    — Part of a longer poem from 1997

Early on in my awakening, about 30 years ago I wrote four blissful pages of poetic discourse of the beginnings of humanity. It is surprisingly familiar as about a year ago, when beginning to explore the origins of angels, humans and God, I happily discovered more pieces to the puzzle.

We existed as one,
Beyond the concept of time and space
Even beyond realm and dimension,
We were part of the universe union / alliance
One being
One had a desire for change
Being so large it split off into five pieces,
One large piece,
Two smaller
And two different mostly intelligence
Of not the same consistency as the other parts.
— Part of the Essence chart 2017

As we now prepare to do something truly magical, adding the secret knowledge of how we came into being back into our consciousness, we make ready a new awakening for our community one which restores power from having hidden knowledge to one of awakened wise elder awareness. We usher in this Aquarian age with truth; beautiful, wondrous, joyous and uplifting.

The knowing of this secret knowledge opens many other doors of knowledge and self-awareness.

Before

Before the time ...

Before the time of legends
Before mythology began
Before elements,
time, space and
matter
I am

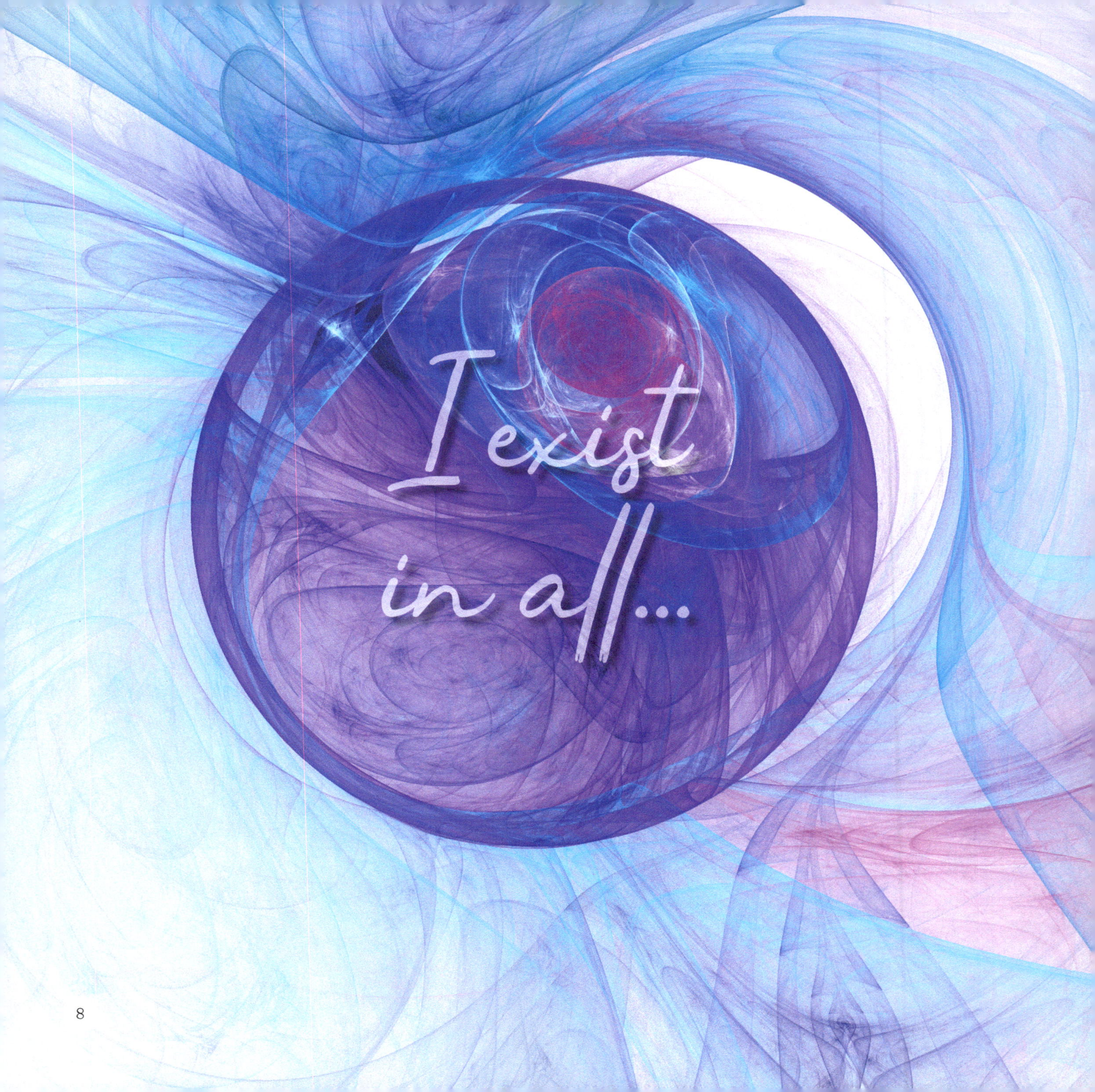

I exist
in all...

I eXist in all
As the very essence of truth
My knowledge is limitless
I am the record of all
I am infinity
I am breath, life, hope, joy
I am surrender
I am all that is pure and true

In truth ...

I eXist not out of some desire
Or will

Rather,
I eXist in truth

You can find me hiding in the
Belly of the biggest lie
I eagerly await
Your discovery

See me ...

As I eXist in everything
Who could not know me?
And yet you gaze past me
Your dearest friend and ally
Your own truth

When you come to me, see me
Truth, clarity, divine vision
Are my fruits

I am the messenger
I am the message

I am all that is and can be
All that is hoped for

Into a oneness ...

Past, present and future blend
Into a oneness
There is no separation

Time and eternity are all and nothing

Weep not my beloved for the echoing
Voice resounds in the heart of the
People who come to me

Come for your healing,
Come for your light
Come for your truth

Come into yourself
I await your recognition
I love, I am you

One

We were a blaze ...

I remember a time when it was not
When all that was
Was what could not be
When who was all
And I was we.

When I eXisted as we
We were a blaze.
The fire was power
The light was life
And I was not
Alone did not eXist

The light
of the we ...

But some part of we broke off
And throwing us out of balance
No longer a single living cell
We scattered in many directions

The brightest parts became the
Stars and planets
Those parts of we that were small
Became less brilliant
Because we could not access all
Of the light of the we

We forgot ...

We became confused
in the spinning off

We became the many

We forgot the we

The self
The sparkle
The glimmer
Became encompassed
by a mass
It had a weight
It moved, thought and felt

What
could
we do?...

It responded to
the temporary
The unreal came
to be the
Unquestioned
truth....
Though we all
knew it was a lie

What could
we do?

I longed for
the we ....

I lacked in spark
My flame grew dangerously small
I longed for the fire of the we
The time of no time
When all was what was not
And no thing was real

I longed for the we
The blaze and the brilliance
The completion.

There is a newness
A beingness
A brightness
Found from the we

*It is
purest
light …*

I in my self
Encompassed by the mass
Lacking in spark
Having glimpsed at the new

It is purest light
Brightest love

The new is the ancient revealed

It is a glimmer of the omni
It is the remembrance of the we
It is the we

Truly in the we ...

I am not
It is not
Truth is that which is unreal

I am and eXist truly in the we
Only in my lack of eXistence
Am I free to be
what is not.

One
Remembered

The self was still...

I remember a time when there was
No speaking
When sound was outside of the realm

The self was still
There was no separation from the great we
We heard the vibrations of the brilliance
We heard the voice of love

Our self responded to the becoming

A time when real was all
And manifest was illusion

The we knew the self fully
The self knew the we

The
silence
and the
ecstasy...

There was no lack
No separateness
Only the echoing vibrations
Of the we

The we were the many
And yet we maintained
The silence and the ecstasy
Of the we

Great gratitude abounded in all parts
Of the we

Joy and peace,
were the stations of our parts

Engulfed
in the
illusion ...

Nirvana, Shangri-la, paradise
Was the home of the we in perfect balance.
The place of the we acknowledged
The place of the we
As the only truth.

And it came to pass

And the we cried for the loss of the selfs
And the selfs knew of the separateness
And the selfs forgot the vibrations of the we

The selfs became engulfed in the illusion
And knew for the first time of the aloneness

Only a
dim memory ....

As the selfs remembered
less and less of the we,
The desires arouse to hang onto
What was manifest.

The attachment to the transient
Became the replacement of the we.

Once strong, brilliant,
The we became only
a dim memory

The holder
of the
flame ...

Many parts of the we
became dangerously dark

And the mother
The great soul of the we
Encompassed each part
So that each tiny flicker would not go out
But would remain enshrined
in her great love

She became the holder of the flame
She whose womb is the gateway
to all the worlds,
Gave with abandon.

Vibrations of the soul ...

She became separate
To each flame her womb became a soul
And so it was.

As a lamp holds the light
So it is the soul holds the spirit.

She held the parts of the we
And though we knew separateness
We could also feel the great mother
Whose memory of the great we
Became protected
In the vibrations of the soul

*It was
safe again...*

The many dangers threatened
To eXtinguish them,
Now clad in its new pelvic armor
It was again safe

And so it was that the great mother
Gave to all, and lost her being
To the save the we
And the we was grateful to the mother
And remembered the time of no time
When all that was was the we.
And so it was.

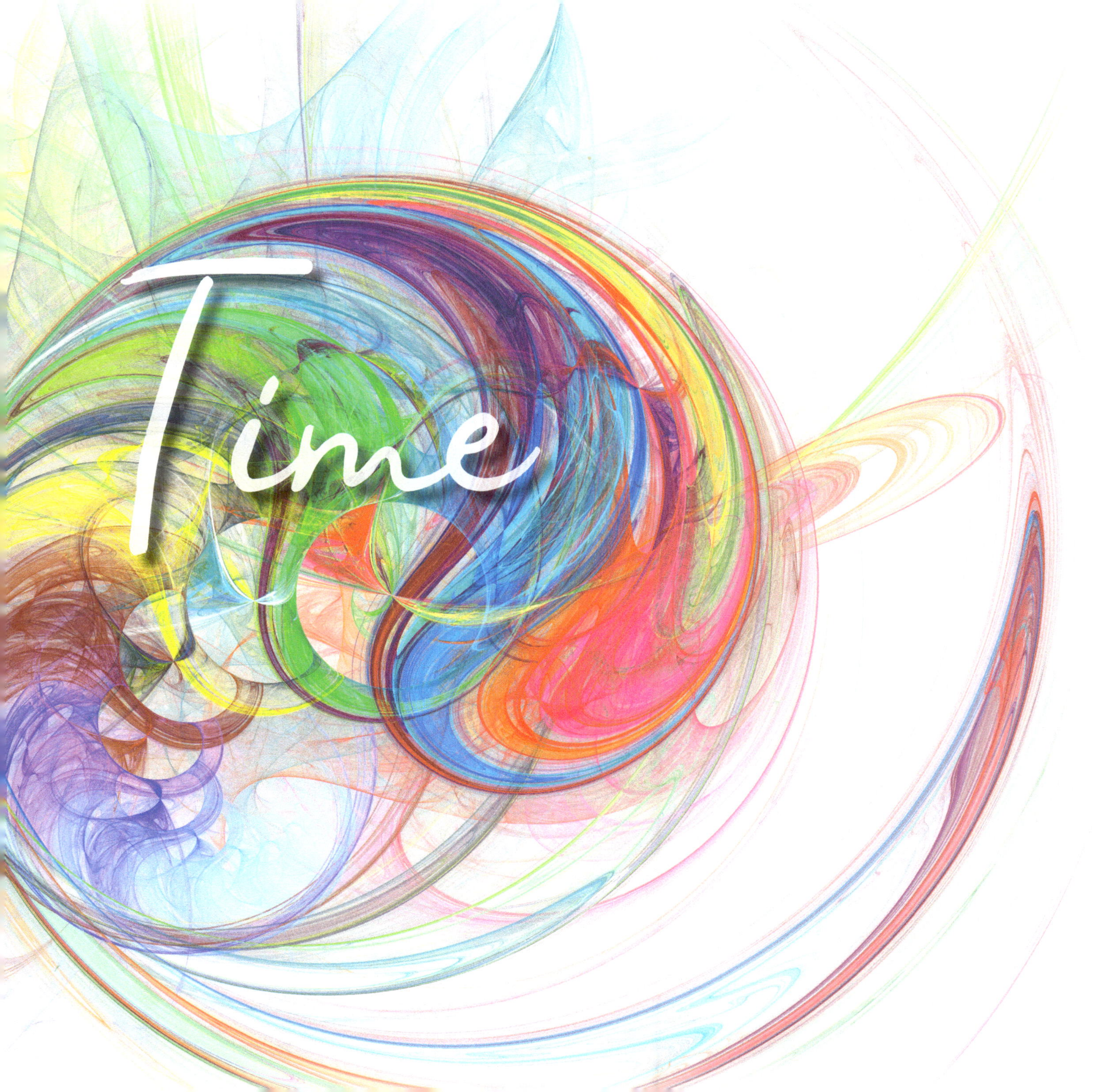
Time

Protect the flame ...

Time
Which became the measure, passed
And the weight and thought encompassing
The flame and soul
Became heavier and darker

And the flame remained safe
In the cradle of the womb
The encompassing weight
Was no longer translucent

As a diamond covered with mud
The selfs remained
And again forgot the we
Though the great mother
Held firmly her stance
To always protect the flame

Her
heart's
call...

Now surrounded in the darkness
Of the weight of what was manifest
She longed for the consort
The love, to light her way

And so it was
Her heart's call was heard through
The we
Through all the worlds
The beloved in his great gratitude
Came to her
And restored her sight

Truth abounded ...

He came for her

She came for all

And so it was the ensouled and ensouler

Bridged by the divine love and truth.

I remember the mother
I remember the coming
I remember the love that embraced my flame

I remember a time when time was not
And all that was was not
Truth abounded

It is hope ...

The vibrations of the we breathing
Were of great ecstasy and joy.

Now remembering gives a new vibration
Not yet as strong as the old
But it is an answer to the call of the we

It is hope

of the
we returned ...

I am the hope
of the we returned
I am the movement and the rest
I am the we surrounded
in the vibrations of truth
That I am not
So then finally I am as the we

As one
breath ...

"Remember," she says,
When we were the I am
No thing could separate us to be we

In the vibrations of all beings
As one breath
As one light
She said,
"Hear the records of this essence
Even before the we
Remember the great I of all."

She calls me
now to her ...

Yes, I remember it well

I hear the call of the great mother
She speaks truth of my origin
Of where I came and must return

She, the armour of my spirit
She calls me now to her.

And so it is.

From the
God Cloud
to Today

the progression and
development of humanity

God Cloud Existing as One

We existed as one, beyond the concept of time and space even beyond realm and dimension, we were part of the universe union/ alliance one being

What caused or what happened in the change?

I ponder consciousness and the presence of great wisdom and intelligence in this chemical mass, for I think it is truly the God Being (s) that brought humans and angels into existence as we once were part of this incredible intelligence and power.

Did we have help in this phase outside of our original parts?

No interferences or interventions in this phase

The First Split to Five Elements

One had a desire for change being so large it split off into five pieces, one large piece, two smaller and two different mostly intelligence of not the same consistency as the other parts.

What caused or what happened in the change?

Without intelligence, the larger piece became a kind of gas. As well the two smaller eventually became a chemical element but the two that were intelligence began to grow and split off morphing gaining and gathering knowledge. The one we called Father/Mother God or Supreme Being came from the second of the different ones, as did angels. The first one grew (was what we would eventually come from) as if in a nursery cared for by the ones who would eventually become angels.

Did we have help in this phase outside of our original parts?

It feels like the God Cloud became too great, too large and needed a new configuration to stabilize. Three other intelligences who had come into existence similar to us nurtured the whole of both, helping us to unify becoming organized and clear.

From the God Cloud to Today
the progression and development of humanity

Human Development

There were 30 steps in this process to becoming spirit and an additional four to becoming human spirit. There are 13 types of human spirit from this source we on earth represent all these types (located on six unique planets).

What caused or what happened in the change?

We moved from intelligence without form to individuated form and function. Although we did not have feeling per say, without a body of course this was an exciting time for us. The first big goal was being individuated spirits. In this phase we were largely perception. Perception sensory emotions, with a strong awareness of feelings, as we individuated had something of a similar nature to thought and we begin to learn to function as individuals.

Did we have help in this phase outside of our original parts?

Of the three other intelligent beings groups one in particular took to the care development and nurturing of human spirit. This group was humanoid, with many similar characteristics to us, helping us as we progressed through many steps. I think quite possibly we began as a science experiment to this group, intelligent beings looking to develop us for perhaps servitude. Later this fully changed, but it was about 17 steps into the process of becoming human, so a great deal of time passed prior to us becoming a real viable, individuated and valued group of intelligent beings. Around this time the first group of developers/scientists left us. We had a great deal of help from God and angels after that. We had a special connection with God and a kind of imprint not DNA but an origin bond, a familiar connection with God who possessed great power, benevolence and wisdom. Angels were farther along in their process and helped us through the next steps of our development to the completion of human spirit.

From the God Cloud to Today
the progression and development of humanity

Angelic Development

Angels had 37 steps to becoming spirit and an additional four to becoming angelic spirit.

What caused or what happened in the change?

15 types of angels from this one source. All of these can be found around the earth (located on 11 planets). Three types of angels can and do live in human bodies type 3, 6 and 8 (these numbers are NOT related to interference numbers, but the 1-15 types of angels)

Did we have help in this phase outside of our original parts?

Both God and other humanoid beings helped progress angelic development. It seems groupings were largely created from the intelligence of the group. It seems knowledge was a factor in becoming the type of angel each grouping was developing into.

From the God Cloud to Today
the progression and development of humanity

God Distinct Identity

God had 4 steps to becoming Great Spirit

What caused or what happened in the change?

There are about 33 of this level of Being

Did we have help in this phase outside of our original parts?

No help was needed

From the God Cloud to Today
the progression and development of humanity

Other Parts of the God Cloud

What caused or what happened in the change?

Without intelligence, the larger piece became a kind of gas. As well the two smaller eventually became a chemical element.

Did we have help in this phase outside of our original parts?

A small part of this continues to exists, while most has disappeared.

About the Author

Julie Renee Doering, Quantum Health Activator, Visionary and Poet awakens a whole new level of awareness and discovery in her visionary poetic and deeply spiritual work.

She is a creative explosion of beauty, truth and awakening and brings a new view and focus to all she does. Her signature is love wisdom. With grace and ease she helps us to know, understand and be more.

As an award winning poet, woman of the year and award recipiant for her gift of leadership, she lives with courage and fortitude. A philanthropist and mother by choice, she champions women and children with a strong faith and commitment to a world elevated by loving understanding and respect.

Author of 12 books. Her spiritual and poetry books include: *Illumination, Breaking Through, Quantum Book of Songs,* and *The Ovarian Rosary.* She is best known for her *Your Divine Human Blueprint* tome. Other books include *100% You Formula, Quantum Healing Secrets, Awakening the Healthy Human,* and *Balance Your Life Now.* And, of course, her precious book *Hello, Goodbye, I Love You Forever.*

Julie Renee can be reached through her website at: www.JulieRenee.com or on any of the following social sites: Facebook, YouTube, LinkedIn, and Twitter.

www.ingramcontent.com/pod-product-compliance
Lightning Source LLC
Chambersburg PA
CBHW060811090426

42737CB00002B/32